Toads and Frogs

Contents

Written by Victoria St John

Introduction

Toads are part of the frog family.
Toads and frogs have cold blood
and live both in water and on land.
They are **amphibians**.
They live in both hot and cold places.

A toad has cold blood and rough skin.

Toad and Frog Bodies

Toads have short, fat bodies.
Frogs are longer and thinner.
Toads' back legs are short,
so they do not jump much.
Frogs' back legs are longer,
so they can jump further.
Toads often have dry, warty skin,
but frogs have smooth, damp skin.

Parts of a Frog

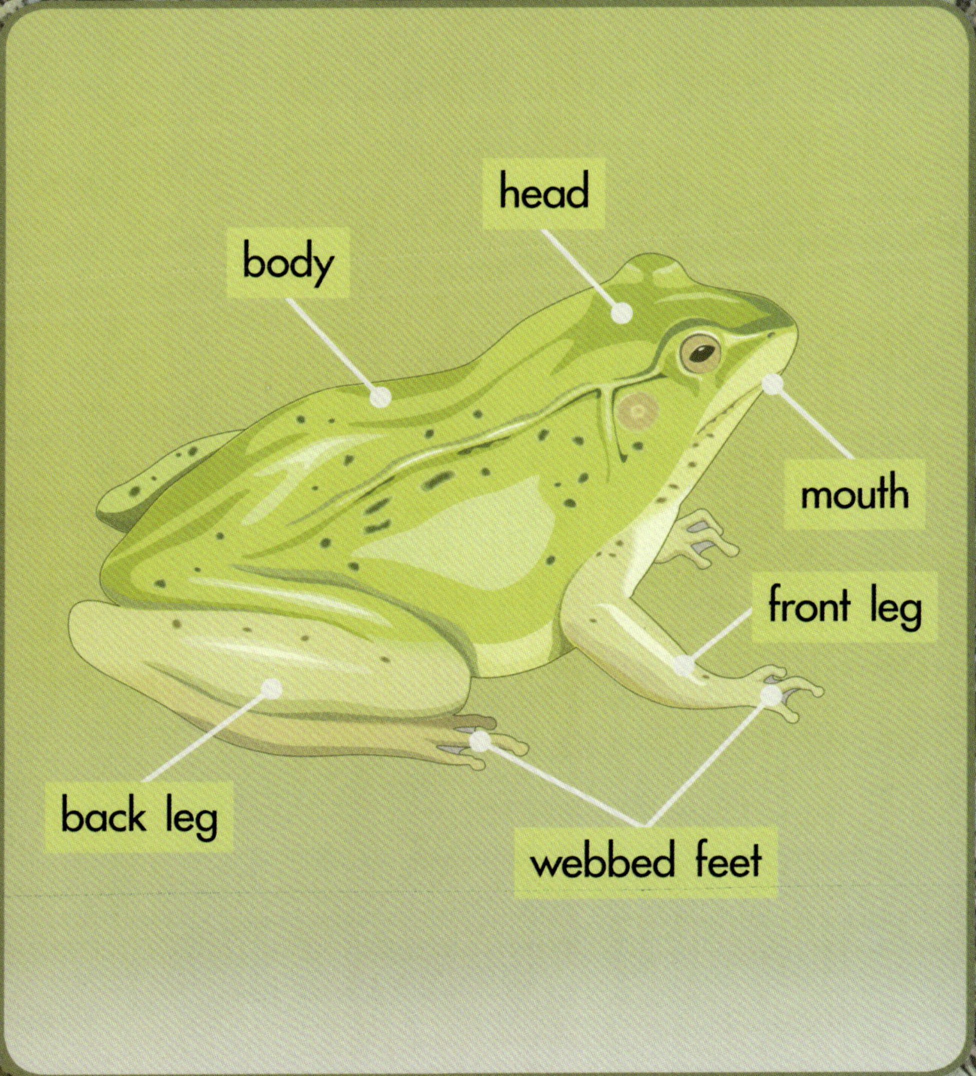

Food

Both toads and frogs eat insects,
slugs, and worms.
Both toads and frogs have a tongue
that they quickly flip out to catch prey.
Toads do not have teeth,
but most frogs do.

A toad eating a worm

Toads and frogs swallow food whole.
They make spit to help them swallow.
They have no bones between their eyes and their mouths.
Their eyes close and sink back and down when they swallow.
This helps push food down their throats.

A tree frog about to swallow a cricket

Night Life

Most toads are active at night,
or **nocturnal**.
Most frogs are nocturnal,
but some are active during the day.
Toads and frogs sleep in grass, trees,
burrows, and leaves.
Some sleep during the cold winter,
or hibernate.

This tree frog looks for food at night.

Eggs and Tadpoles

Most toads and frogs lay eggs in water.
Toads lay eggs in long, jelly-like strings.
Frogs lay eggs in clusters.
Tadpoles hatch from toads'
and frogs' eggs.

This tadpole will soon grow front legs and its tail will shrink.

Tadpoles have parts
that let them breathe underwater,
or **gills**, and a tail to help them swim.
They lose the gills and tail
as they grow bigger.
Instead, they grow two legs on each side.
Eventually, they grow into toads or frogs.

Life Cycle of a Frog

Keeping Safe

Toads have ways to keep safe.
They have poison glands on their head.
The poison keeps them safe
from animals that hunt them, or **predators**.
Toads can puff themselves up
to frighten predators.
Some frogs have poison, but most do not.

Poisonous skin helps protect this frog from predators.

Cane Toads

Cane toads come from South America.
They can be 15 cm long,
or a bit longer than a pen.
They can weigh 2 kg,
or as much as four tubs of butter.
People first brought these amphibians
to Australia to control cane beetles.
Now, they are pests.
They have no predators here
and endanger other animals.

A cane toad can poison pets and native animals.

Goliath Frogs

Goliath frogs live in West Africa.
They are the biggest frogs on Earth.
These amphibians can be 30 cm long and weigh 3 kg.
They are not pests.
They are an endangered species.

A goliath frog lives in a rainforest.

Threats to Toads and Frogs

Many toads and frogs are in danger.
People destroy places where they live.
Pollution affects places where they breed.
A fungus is killing them, too.

Toads and frogs are alike in many ways.

Glossary

amphibians – animals with cold blood that spend part of their life in water and part of their life on land

gills – parts on the sides of a tadpole that allow it to breathe underwater

nocturnal – active at night

predators – animals that hunt other animals

Index